How My Family Came to Be —
Daddy, Papa and Me

Andrew R. Aldrich
Illustrated by Mike Motz

A New Family Press Book

for Nehemiah,
and other kids lucky enough to have
both a Daddy and a Papa…

I am deeply grateful to the following family, friends, colleagues and other generous contributors for their time, encouragement and expertise throughout this project.

Nehemiah Kirkley Aldrich; Sandy Brumbaum; Jay and Joan Butler; Anne Cadigan; Betty DeGeneres; Stephanie Engelmann; Margaret Grover; Elaine Herscher; Frederick Hertz; Jennifer Hughes; Lisa Key and Valory Mitchell; John Kirkley; Brian Lewis and Peter Cleaveland; Chris ("Aunt Chili") Maddox; Rocky Morrison; Mike Motz; Dan Savage; Susan Stutzman; Johnny Symons; Loretta Weaks; Marguerite Wright

—A.A.

1st printing

New Family Press, 389 Belmont Street Suite 105, Oakland, CA 94610, USA
Visit us at www.newfamilypress.com

Book design and layout
Ruth Marcus, Sequim, WA, Email: Rmarcus@olypen.com

Library of Congress Control Number : 2003093757

ISBN 0-9742008-0-8

Printed in Korea

The day I was born was a *happy* day.

My birth mom was too sick to take care of children,
but Daddy and Papa wanted a baby *just like me*!

Daddy and Papa met with a lady called a social worker and asked her to help them find a baby to adopt.

She made sure that Daddy and Papa were nice
and that our house was safe for a baby.

There was *lots and lots* of paperwork for them to fill out.
They also learned how to keep me safe and healthy.

And Daddy and Papa got ready for *fun*!

One day Daddy and Papa got a telephone call
from the social worker.
She told them all about me.

Daddy and Papa were excited.
They were also nervous since they were
going to meet their new baby – *me*!

When we met, I ran up to Daddy and Papa
and said, "Ga!"

Daddy and Papa said they loved me from the minute they saw me and wanted for all of us to be a family.

A few days later, they picked me up
and brought me home.

My room was filled with
toys and clothes and books.

And my home was filled with love –
from my *forever* family.

One time in the middle of the night I woke up crying because a new tooth was growing in my mouth.

Daddy ran down the hall
and into my room to comfort me.
Papa got me medicine to make the hurt go away.

Families help each other
because they are made up of people
who *love* you.

I have lots of women
who help raise me too – like my teachers,
my godmother, and my granny.

And my friends are all kinds –
young, old, boys, girls, with one mom, or two dads,
or just plain old one mom and one dad.

We play, talk, read, hug and sometimes fight,
just like other families.
I love my Daddy and Papa with all my heart.